BLESSINGS
in
DISGUISE

BLESSINGS
in
DISGUISE

*The journey of two souls and how they
both heal together in the most unusual way.*

ELI K. ANYADI

XULON PRESS

Xulon Press
2301 Lucien Way #415
Maitland, FL 32751
407.339.4217
www.xulonpress.com

Paperback ISBN-13: 978-1-66282-304-6
Ebook ISBN-13: 978-1-66282-305-3

DEDICATION

To my wife, Alicia
Thank you for your love and support
To Nii Amar Amarfio
Thank you for believing in me

TABLE OF CONTENTS

PREFACE

GROWING UP, MY FATHER LOVED TO TELL STORIES OF his childhood and personal experiences. He chose which ones to tell as and when he saw it fit given the circumstances. His stories always sought to encourage, chastise, correct, guide, and uplift. I have found over the years that those same stories he told repeatedly have stuck with me and become my moral compass for navigating through life and inspiration whenever I need it. In these difficult and uncertain times, we need to be reminded of how much God cares and hasn't given up on us, and I see no better way to do that than to share a story that reflects this truth. Just like my father, I also like to use stories to tell my truths. I guess the apple doesn't fall far from the tree! The events in this book are based on true circumstances and will inspire and encourage you no matter where you are in life. They will also challenge your perspective on what you have always thought God's blessings looked like. Like what my father's stories did for me over the years, I am hopeful the story you are about to read may for many years serve as a reminder that God still has a plan to bless and deliver you, even if it doesn't look like it.

Introduction

MANY OF US ARE UNCONSCIOUSLY ACCUSTOMED TO A particular way that God works. This is usually based on our understanding of how God operates and from our personal experiences with Him. If God helps us through a certain source or delivers us from a situation in a certain way, we tend to think that the next time we are in need, His help or deliverance will come through the same way. Even though it may seem that way, this is not always the case.

> *"For My thoughts are not your thoughts, nor are your ways My ways," declares the LORD. "For as the heavens are higher than the earth, so are My ways higher than your ways and My thoughts higher than your thoughts." — Isaiah 55:8-9 (AMP)*

Isaiah 55:8-9 goes beyond saying that there is no putting God in a box. God may have shown His deeds to the people of Israel, but He showed His ways to Moses (Psalm

107:7). In the book of Exodus 33:13, Moses prayed: "If you are pleased with me, teach me your ways so I may know You and continue to find favor with You." The key word here is "teach." Until God teaches you His ways, you will not continue to find favor with Him. Moses recognized this. God's ways need to be taught because they are never the same. Where you once found favor with God may be different the next time, and not knowing this will cause you to miss out on opportunities to be blessed.

Now to buttress this point, let's look at a few unlikely ways that God has healed and delivered people:

1. Jesus Heals a Man Born Blind

> *"When He had said this, He spat on the ground and made mud with His saliva, and He spread the mud [like an ointment] on the man's eyes. And He said to him, 'Go, wash in the pool of Siloam' (which is translated, Sent). So, he went away and washed, and came back seeing." — John 9:6-7 (AMP)*

Now, this has to be one of my favorite miracles that Jesus performed in the Bible simply because it defies every logical reasoning I could apply to justify this healing as possible. Understand that by nature, the eye in itself is designed to repel any foreign material that gets on it or in it. It does this through the shedding of tears, which helps remove foreign materials, and through natural reflexes. We all tend to blink fast when something gets close to our eyes or we rub them until the foreign material is removed. But here, the very thing the eye is designed to repel is what Jesus used to bring healing to it.

2. Rahab and the Spies

> *"But the woman had taken the two men and hidden them; so, she said, 'Yes, two men came to me, but I did not know where they were from. When it was time to close the [city] gate at dark, the men left; I do not know where they went. Pursue them quickly, for [if you do] you will overtake them.'" — Joshua 2:4-5 (AMP)*

A little background history to this story—Joshua secretly sent two spies to survey the land, one part of which was Jericho. The spies went and hid themselves in the house of a prostitute named Rahab. The king of Jericho, having knowledge of this, inquired with Rahab about the spies, but she lied and covered up for them. Here, the story gets interesting. Rahab let the spies in on some information that later confirmed their victory over Jericho. She said, "I know the Lord has given you this land and that, a great fear of you has fallen on us. So that all who live in this country are melting in fear because of you" (Joshua 2:9). All of the information the spies came looking for was delivered to them by God through a prostitute. We know this because the spies reported the same words back to Joshua as confirmation of victory over Jericho, saying, "The Lord has surely given the whole land into our hands; all the people are melting in fear because of us" (Joshua 2:24). What an unlikely source to find such vital information!

3. Jacob's Dream

> *"Then Jacob awoke from his sleep and he said, 'Without any doubt the* Lord *is in this place, and I did not realize it.'"* — *Genesis 28:16 (AMP)*

How many times have we expected God to show up in certain places but He doesn't? I know I have been there many times! When He does not show up when I expect Him to, in my frustration and desperation, I keep asking myself over and over again if I prayed enough or was righteous enough or if God is mad at me...questions I now know have no bearing on God's willingness to help me. Jacob laid his head on a stone for a pillow, which certainly can be agreed to be a hard place and not somewhere you would think God would show up. Jacob clearly did not expect to meet God at such a hard and difficult place, but when he awoke from his sleep, he came to the realization that God had been there all along—he just didn't know it. Jacob later went on to describe the place, saying, "How awesome is this place! This is none other than the house of God, and this is the gate of heaven" (Genesis 28:17). What an unusual place for God to show up and what an unusual place to be described as the house of God!

Like the story of the blind man, what if God used what you repel most to bring you healing? Like the story of Rahab, what if God used the most unlikely person to set up your victory over those who seek to destroy you? And like Jacob, what if God shows up where you least expect Him to? Come with me, and let's journey into the lives of Kwami and Bailey and how they both heal together in the most unusual way.

CHAPTER I

TRIP ABROAD

ON THE 25TH OF AUGUST, 2015, KWAMI, A TWENTY-SEVen-year-old man of Ghanaian descent lands at Denver International Airport at approximately 9:30 am. His first time travelling outside of Ghana, West Africa, he is completely amazed by the magnitude as well as the splendor of the airport. As he carries on observing his environment, his eyes can't help but notice the stringent security detail all around him. There are cameras at every corner and security personnel pacing up and down with sniffing dogs, a couple of which have gone past him couple of times. This takes his memory back to a television show he had seen many times before titled *Border Security*. With each episode he had watched, the more his fears and concerns about travelling had heightened, especially after watching episodes that showed people being fined and deported for their ignorance of the law. These reflections alone get him panicky, as you can tell by his candid expressions and the premeditated steps he takes, walking as though he is on thin ice. With so many different signs indicating where to go, Kwami figures out where he ought to be and gets done with all of the lengthy airport formalities with ease. He spots an empty taxi cab that is prepared to take him to Colorado Heights University, where he will be a resident for the next two years. Settling down in school entails enrolling for classes and getting through a three-day orientation process, which he completes successfully. Settled in, he does a quick check on how much money he has left to spend and is startled to discover that $600 of his $1,000 spending money has been used up. He has had to foot the bill for an additional course that wasn't covered by his tuition fees. He has twenty-three months to go and $400 to his name. Kwami reckons the only way to live through these twenty-three months is to get a job. But where? He has no clue. He goes on a job hunt online and applies to a Chick-Fil-A restaurant two hours away from his dorm. No later than a week, he gets a call to come in for an interview. He is thrilled, but he dreads taking up the position because it's illegal to work outside of campus as an international student. This is a tough spot for Kwami—he is torn between survival and complying with the law. Each one of his friends who are international students have jobs outside of campus, and as a result are better off financially than he is. Kwami, considering his options, of which he has very few, concludes that getting a job is the only way he is going to be able to get by.

He is up 5:00 am, gets through his morning routine, and out he goes, geared up to take the first of three buses and walk another twenty minutes to the Chick-Fil-A. He is not amused by the cold and falling snow; however, that isn't going to stop him from getting to the restaurant. Snowing outside at a temperature of -1 degree, he suddenly gets a notification on his phone. Two of the three buses he will be commuting on are running late. Freezing and shivering to the bone, he is determined to wait for the buses in spite of the extended delay. Four hours late, he makes it to the restaurant with numb feet and fingers. The interview starts immediately, and he is finished within thirty minutes. Filling out paperwork and reading through training manuals follows after, which takes another forty minutes to complete. Shortly after, he is required to complete a quiz. Fortunately, it is nothing he can't handle. Undeterred by the weather, he makes it back to the dorm ecstatic about his new job. The journey takes barely two hours. His commute was much shorter this time, surprisingly. However, all while he was on the bus, he was working out how much money he would use up on groceries, clothes, his phone bill, and other miscellaneous expenses. Based on his calculations, an hourly rate of ten dollars over a thirty-hour-week schedule should bring in enough money to go around.

He feels pretty good about this and can't wait to start work. *Well, why not?* he thinks and decides to celebrate with a bottle of red wine and a three-course dinner. This means spending a quarter of what is left of his money. Nonetheless, that doesn't bother him as he is going to earn it back anyway.

The weekend ended, his first day of work is here. He is assigned an early bird roster, which means he has to leave his dorm at 4:00 am if he is going to make it on time. He gets there at approximately 6:30 am. Thirty minutes late, he is put to work instantly. He is initially posted to the kitchen, where he is taught how to wash pans and clean vegetables. He also deep-fries everything from chicken nuggets to potato fries to chicken patties. In the subsequent days, his fingers are put to work putting together all the various sandwiches expeditiously in response to numerous drive-thru orders. It is not difficult to spot Kwami in the restaurant. He is identifiably the only male of color staff member, which makes him careful to be a very astute worker, keeping away from confrontation as much as he can.

It's the end of the week and time for the restaurant to restock. Perceiving that he is physically capable, Kwami is called on to join up with two other colleagues to offload food items from a delivery truck. He carries as many as he can, hoping to make a good impression on his supervisor, John, who is watching from a distance. The truck driver, a white, middle-aged, full-bearded man, grabs the last bit of groceries from his truck.

"Where are you from?" he asks while handing over the box of groceries to Kwami.

"Ghana," Kwami replies.

"Where in Ghana do you live?" the truck driver proceeds to ask.

"I live in Accra," Kwami answers.

"Cool…I know Accra and Kumasi," the truck driver smiles. "I knew a guy from Ghana. He sold shoes would send a truckload of them to the port to be shipped to Ghana. I was usually the truck driver. Very nice guy and hard-working—I liked him. How long have you been working here?"

"It's been just a week," says Kwami, looking and listening over his shoulders to make sure he is not wanted inside.

The truck driver leans forward toward Kwami and whispers, "Do you like it here?"

"Yes, sir, I do," Kwami answers back confidently.

The truck driver reaches out for a handshake, and Kwami meets him halfway, after which Kwami does a quick dash back into the restaurant. John then comes out of the restaurant to have a few last words with the truck driver.

"We got everything?" John throws the question to the truck driver.

"Yep! Pretty much," the truck driver responds, taking a second look in the truck.

"You know the guy from Ghana, the black dude? He is a good guy. The guys from Ghana are very hardworking. You have got a good one," he continues in his reply.

Kwami, lucky to have heard the truck driver's kind words about him, can't help but smile as he leans on the back door of the restaurant. He was initially going back out to see if the truck driver needed anymore help, but upon hearing his remarks about him, he decides to stay back and eavesdrop on the rest of the conversation. He feels that God has inspired the truck driver's words as a sign that Kwami is exactly where God wants him to be. This definitely changes Kwami's demeanor at work over the coming weeks. He works with a lot more confidence, and soon enough, he becomes very comfortable with his work colleagues. He thinks to himself, *This is what I will be doing for the rest of my time here in America.* Well, things don't quite work out that way...

Doctor's Appointment

It's almost the end of the year, and Bailey, a four-year-old white girl and the only child of Mr. and Mrs. Taylor, has to pay a visit to her pediatrician for her wellness check-up. On the 13th of December at 8:30 am, Mr. and Mrs. Taylor show up at Children's Hospital Colorado, ready to meet Dr. Nord for Bailey's appointment. Dr. Nord has been Bailey's pediatrician for the past four years. His receptionist has them sit and wait for about five minutes.

"Dr. Nord will see you now," she tells Mr. and Mrs. Taylor, ushering them into his office.

"How are you, Mr. and Mrs. Taylor?" Dr. Nord asks, extending a handshake to both of them, "and how is Bailey doing?"

"Very well, thanks, Doc. Bailey is doing well too. We are here for her wellness check-up," Mr. Taylor replies.

"Very well! Let's get started then," Dr. Nord responds.

Dr. Nord walks around his table, holds onto Bailey's hand, and takes her into an examination room right next to his office. After twenty minutes, Bailey comes back out with Dr. Nord with peppermint candy in her hand. She runs back into her mom's arms with a smile on her face.

"Bailey looks very healthy—nothing to worry about. Just make sure she is eating her fruits and vegetables and drinking a lot of water," Dr. Nord says, looking directly at both parents.

"Thanks, Doc, that's really good to know. In that case, are we all cleared to leave now?" Mr. Taylor asks.

"Yes, you are. You are welcome to call me and stop by anytime you have any concerns about Bailey's health," Dr. Nord replies.

Just then, Mr. and Mrs. Taylor turn to look each other in the eye as though they have something more to say but are unsure if they should. They both stand up, thank Dr. Nord, and walk out of his office. As they walk past the waiting area, about to open the door to the main entrance of the hospital, Mrs. Taylor whispers to her husband, "Honey! We need to talk to Doc about it; maybe he can help us."

"You are right, honey," says Mr. Taylor after he turns to look at Bailey.

Mr. Taylor walks to the receptionist and politely says, "Hi, Julia, we would like to have a few last words with Doc if he is not busy."

Fortunately for them, Dr. Nord's next appointment is not until another hour. Julia kindly walks them into Dr. Nord's office again.

"Mr. and Mrs. Taylor! I hope everything is okay?" Dr. Nord exclaims, standing up, surprised to see them back in his office.

"Actually, no, Doc, it isn't! We have a major concern about Bailey's mental health, and we do not know what to do," Mrs. Taylor tells Dr. Nord.

"Okay! Not a problem. I know somebody who could be of great help to you," Dr. Nord says, handing them a contact card for a child psychologist.

Mrs. Taylor grabs onto it firmly with a sign of relief on her face, as though she has just gotten some good news.

"Thank you so much, Doc. This means so much to us. We will be sure to contact her as soon as tomorrow," Mr. Taylor says.

With great optimism, Mr. and Mrs. Taylor walk out of Dr. Nord's office.

CHAPTER 2

THE STRUGGLE IS REAL

KWAMI HAS SPENT THREE WEEKS WORKING AT CHICK-Fil-A. One morning, as soon as John gets to work, he calls Kwami in for a short meeting. Kwami wonders what could have led to this impromptu meeting that cannot wait until his shift is over and becomes concerned. Trying to imagine what the meeting might be about, Kwami begins to mentally check off a list of great qualities he brings to the table at work. *I have been working hard. God inspired a truck driver to say good things about me. I have a good working relationship with my colleagues. What could possibly go wrong?* he thinks.

"Kwami! How are you doing today?" John asks, pulling a chair closer to his side.

"Pretty good, came in on time like always and went straight to work," Kwami answers with shaking lips.

"Good. We admire your work ethic. You work well with the rest of the team, and that is what is important to us," John says.

Kwami, feeling assertive after hearing John praise him, says, "Well, thank you, John. I have…"

But before he can finish his sentence, John cuts in.

"Kwami, we have one problem though. We have tried validating your employment eligibility, but that has proved futile over the past two weeks. As part of our company policy, we need to make sure all of our staff are eligible for employment."

Kwami, caught off guard by this, looks at John, very confused.

"Are you sure you are eligible to work?" John continues to ask. "Otherwise, that is going to be a big problem."

"John, I will be honest with you. I am only eligible to work on campus. I took this job because I have no money to look after myself for the rest of my stay in America," Kwami answers with a sad look.

"Kwami, that is a big problem. I am sorry, but we are going to have to let you go. If we insist on you staying, you are going to be in big trouble with the law," John says.

"I understand, John. I will leave right away," Kwami says with a down demeanor.

Kwame proceeds to leave the office. He changes out of his work clothes, hands them over to John, and tells his work colleagues that he is done for the day. He heads home on the cold winter morning, never to return to the restaurant again. His twenty-minute walk to the bus station feels like a good forty minutes. As he walks back with his head tucked under his jacket, trying to protect his face from the falling snow, he reflects on how he thought he was very lucky to have had such a job, despite it being two hours away. But on a second thought, he is glad he doesn't have to make the journey anymore. He thinks of the delivery truck driver and his kind words; unfortunately, they could not save him. Kwami, absentminded at this point, slips on black ice and falls flat on his butt. "Ouch!" he yells out in pain. Out of frustration, he lashes out, speaking pidgin English, "Like I dey Ghana this thing no go happen me. Sake of Cho see how man dey suffer... mtchew!" Speaking to himself at the bus station, he says, "Maybe I should call my parents to send me money?" He only made $200 from the first two weeks of working at the restaurant, which he used to pay his phone bill and go grocery shopping. Unfortunately, that brings him right back to where he started. "Never mind," he says to himself. "They are already carrying the burden of my tuition."

Kwami gets to his dorm highly disappointed and angry at himself for taking a job off campus, especially knowing its implications. With very little money, he is sure he is going to go through some days with no food.

To make sure the little he has will last as long as possible, he eats his lunch and dinner from a Chinese restaurant right across the street called the Great Wall Chinese Express. They have a buffet menu that goes for $1.35 per scoop. Kwami usually spends $10 a day at the restaurant, $5 in the afternoon and $5 in the evening. He is committed to this budget. He goes there so much that the old Chinese lady, probably in her sixties, who serves and attends to customers gives him food on credit when he has no money. But twenty-one months is a long time to live off her benevolence.

HELP IS HERE, OR IS IT?

Mr. and Mrs. Taylor make an appointment to meet Mrs. Hall, the child psychologist recommended to them by Dr. Nord. Prior to setting up the meeting, Mr. and Mrs. Taylor stay up many nights counting every dollar they anticipate they will have to pay for Mrs. Hall's services, whose rates they found on her private practice website. They know Bailey's fears are not going to leave in a day; that, however, means many more sessions with Mrs. Hall and a lot of money to be spent. They almost gave up the idea of meeting Mrs. Hall, considering how expensive it was going to be, but the thought of Bailey, their child, whom they loved so much, was enough to motivate them to spend all that they had to help her.

The day of the appointment is here, and Mr. and Mrs. Taylor are five minutes early. They immediately walk up to the woman at the front desk.

"Hello, ma'am. We are Mr. and Mrs. Taylor, and I believe we have a 10:00 am appointment with Mrs. Hall," says Mr. Taylor.

"Yes! I believe you do. Hi, my name is Kaelin. Welcome, Mr. and Mrs. Taylor. Have a seat for me. Mrs. Hall will have you come in shortly," Kaelin says.

"Sure!" Mr. Taylor replies.

They find a seat in the waiting area and sit, waiting for their turn. They see quite a number of kids with their parents waiting to be seen as well. Automatically, they both assume that Mrs. Hall must be a really good child psychologist. This makes them feel more confident about Mrs. Hall and her ability to help Bailey.

"Ready, Mr. and Mrs. Taylor!" Kaelin yells out from her desk.

"Yes, we sure are," Mr. Taylor responds quickly.

Kaelin directs them to Mrs. Hall's office, which is right behind her desk station.

"Good morning, Mrs. Hall," Mr. Taylor says, extending a handshake.

"Good morning, Mr. and Mrs. Taylor, and good morning to Bailey," Mrs. Hall responds, shaking both Mr. and Mrs. Taylor's hands.

"Say hi to Mrs. Hall, Bailey," Mrs. Taylor whispers to Bailey, who is sitting on her lap.

"Hi," Bailey says with a wave.

"Thank you for having us. Dr. Nord is Bailey's pediatrician, and he recommended we see you concerning Bailey, so that's why we're here," Mr. Taylor says boldly, leaning forward.

"Great! Dr. Nord is a good pediatrician and a personal friend too. We go way back in our college days at the University of Colorado. Well, let's get to it. What seems to be the problem with Bailey?" Mrs. Hall asks.

"Growing up, Bailey was always very bright, smart, happy, playful, confident, and fearless. But we have noticed a sudden change in her behavior. She will cry about anything and everything and hates going out to the park or playing with her friends, which is not like her at all. We can't get her to do anything. She can't sleep with the lights off and will not try anything fun and new. We are afraid this fear is holding her back from developing and being the wonderful kid she is. We certainly don't want her to miss out on life because of her fears," Mrs. Taylor narrates.

"Has she been exposed to any form of abuse?" Mrs. Hall asks with a suspicious look.

"Absolutely not! We have never laid a finger on her, if that is what you are insinuating," Mrs. Taylor responds defensively.

"Alright, then I can tell you now that there is nothing more to worry about. She is still very young. Just give it time, and it will all go away. Time is all you need," Mrs. Hall says, looking away.

"Mrs. Hall, are you saying we should do nothing and hope with time that Bailey will get better?" Mrs. Taylor responds, shocked.

"That is what I am saying," Mrs. Hall responds authoritatively.

Mr. and Mrs. Taylor look at each other in shock and disappointment. They can't believe what they have just heard. They rise up from their seats and get ready to step out.

"Thank you, Mrs. Hall. We understand. We will not waste any more of your time. We will be leaving now," Mr. Taylor says.

"I wish Bailey and your family well," Mrs. Hall says as she gets up and escorts them to the door.

Mr. and Mrs. Taylor leave Mrs. Hall's office in haste and storm out of the building. They sit still in their car for a while without moving. Staring into the open, they both burst into tears with their hands covering their mouths. Mr. Taylor grabs Mrs. Taylor's hand firmly, who at this point is sobbing uncontrollably. They try to be as quiet as possible, but they notice Bailey watching them, so they quickly get themselves together.

Chapter 3

Sunny Days, Better Days

THE WINTER SEASON IS GRADUALLY WITHERING AWAY. The long chilly nights are now shorter and warmer. The trees appear as though they have been given a new soul as fresh green leaves begin to sprout out of their branches. This, however, does not translate to a new sparkle for Kwami. Two things still linger on—Kwami has no money and no job. There have been many evenings that he didn't have money to buy a meal; nevertheless, he has not gone to bed without one, except this particular Sunday evening. The old lady from the Great Wall Chinese Express who he affectionately calls "Mother" and on whose benevolence he depends on for his evening meals on credit, has, unluckily for him, been replaced by a much younger lady. She is obviously unfamiliar with Kwami's dilemma, so there is no counting on a meal that night. Without having eaten anything the whole day, Kwami is very weak, miserable, and unhappy with his life. He has never been in a situation like this before. Curled up in bed with sunken eyes, he reminisces of all the pleasant phases of his life in Ghana, singling out a unique memory of his grandmother cooking his beloved meal of rice balls with peanut soup, which she would do every Sunday. He had always looked forward to Sundays because of her. Even though she had passed on, he could never forget her.

At midnight, Kwami wakes up from a cold sweat. Fearing he might be getting sick, he quickly goes to freshen up. Still very hungry, Kwami sits on his bed and considers the reality of his situation. He realizes that he has to do something— otherwise, he can forget about eating for the next twenty months! This is a rude awakening for him as he never imagined being in such a situation in America.

Kwami is determined to find a solution. He starts off with what he knows to do but hasn't done in a while. He goes on his knees and prays to God.

"Father, who art in heaven, thank you for grace and mercy and everything else I am not deserving of. Father, I am even more grateful for my circumstance at this very moment. I know You know my current state and all that I have been through recently. I just have one request. I am going to try to get another job. I believe there is a job out there that will help me meet my daily needs. Lead me to that job, Lord. In

Jesus's name, I pray. Thank you, Lord. Amen!" Kwami prays out loud with an authoritative voice.

Kwami begins to feel resilient afterward in a way he has never experienced before. He stays up until dawn, giving the search for a job another try. At long last, he finds a job he thinks he can do. It is a lifeguard position at a swim school thirty minutes away. He applies for the position and retreats back to bed, optimistic about his chances of getting it. The coming weeks are challenging, but he feeds off the kindness of some of his friends he has made in school.

One thing that keeps coming back to Kwami after that night is the desire to start going back to church. He finds a church to attend the following Sunday that is a branch from his church back home in Ghana. The service undeniably feels like home. The singing, dancing, and sermon are exact replicas of what he is used to. Once church ends, he is called over for a first timers meeting. During these meetings, the church leaders usually try to find out more about the new visitors and extend a warm welcome with drinks and food. The food certainly catches Kwami's attention, but everything is about to take a different turn for him.

When the church leaders find out how long his commute is to church as well as his current struggles, they are determined to get him a car to use while he is in America. A lady who is present at the meeting suggests offering a vacant car in her possession to Kwami to use at no cost. He can't believe it! When the meeting is finished, Kwami gets an email notification on his phone from the new job he applied to. They want him to come in the next day, Monday, for an interview.

LEAP OF FAITH

It's the summer holidays. Bailey's mom and dad are really hoping this summer does not end up like the last. The preceding summer, Bailey declined anything that got her out of the house. She even turned down camping with her friends. This was disturbing for her parents as summer camp used to be Bailey's preferred interest. Nonetheless, one thing that has remained constant is Bailey's love for water. She loves to have fun in the water; hence, her mum and dad decided to sign her up for swim lessons. Bailey appeared keen about the idea, so her parents were hopeful something good would come out of it. Ultimately, being able to get her to do something outside the house was a major development for her parents, and Bailey adored her new swimsuit and goggles.

It's the first day of swim lessons. Bailey seems eager; her parents, on the other hand, appear anxious yet hopeful. She paces to class with a grin on her face, joining her new swim mates. Her turn is delayed while her classmates each have a go. Finally, it's time for her turn, but she freaks out. Shoving away her swim instructor, she begins to tear up and murmur her discomfort.

"Be quiet! There is no crying in my class. That's what the little kids do. You are a big kid, so hush!" her swim instructor yells while gripping Bailey's arms firmly.

Terrified, Bailey stops weeping right away. The swim instructor opts to give the others a go a second time while Bailey hangs on. Almost immediately, it is Bailey's turn again. This time, the swim instructor doesn't give her an opportunity to object. He forcefully clutches her arms, dragging her to the middle of the pool. Instantly, he drops her, and she quickly begins to go under. He does a six-second count, after which, he yanks her back up.

"You have to listen!" he yells once more.

Bailey, upon reaching the surface of the water, lets out a howl of fear and begins to tremble fiercely. Alarmed by her reaction, the swim instructor tries to console her. *Bang!* The door that connects the parents to the pool deck opens. Next come Bailey's parents dashing to snatch her out of the pool. They seize her from the swim instructor and put a towel around her, then take her to shower and get dressed. Together with Bailey, they hasten off to the front desk, demanding to have a word with the supervisor on duty.

"This is the worst swim school ever!" Mrs. Taylor shouts at the supervisor, whose office she breaks into without a knock.

Startled, the supervisor tries to uncover what's going on. Efforts to calm Mrs. Taylor down nonetheless prove futile.

"Your swim instructor just sank my baby girl in your pool and pretended nothing happened! This is not what we signed up for!" Mrs. Taylor continues shouting.

The supervisor perceives how serious Mrs. Taylor's grievances are and promises she will get to the bottom of it and give Bailey all the support she will need moving forward.

"Thank you, but your help won't be needed," Mr. Taylor says graciously. "We are withdrawing Bailey from this swim school."

Mr. and Mrs. Taylor lash out at each other on their drive back home for even proposing the idea of a swim school. They hold themselves liable for what appears to now be another traumatic experience for Bailey. In spite of what has taken place, Mrs. Taylor is fixed on making an appearance at her women's fellowship meeting later that night. She has been a member of the group since the beginning of Bailey's predicament and has felt the most empathy here than anywhere else. Tonight, Mrs. Taylor has resolved to vent out all the negative emotions she has suppressed for as far back as her childhood.

Mr. Taylor chauffeurs her to the meeting. Typically, the women are given the platform to share any worries they may have, after which, help through prayer or any form of assistance is suggested and offered. Mrs. Taylor whispers to the fellowship leader that she has something on her mind she would like to voice out. Sharing time begins, and first to go is Mrs. Taylor, who is brought to the podium. Before she utters a word, she inhales intensely, coupled with a soft exhale afterwards.

"This has to be the most difficult thing I have ever done. I am here because I have a story to tell, a story that I have never told anyone. You're all familiar with my daughter's predicament—how reserved, fearful, and timid she has become within the past two years. Only, today, things took a turn for the worse. My baby girl just had a traumatizing experience at a swim school and may never get to do the one thing she loves most. Well, what a lot people do not know is that I was just like Bailey. At the very same age, I began to experience an unhealthy fear of things. This escalated so much that I was diagnosed with chronic fear. It robbed me of my whole life. I could hardly do anything without feeling some form of anxiety…I couldn't go to sports games, neither could I go to concerts with large crowds. I also always felt insecure in my relationships. I missed out on many opportunities that came my way. I wish I had had someone who cared enough to notice what was going on with me and tell me how much of life I was losing out on. Now my baby girl is going through the exact same thing. I am afraid that life is going to pass her by, just as it did in my case. I have done all that I can do, but things only get worse with time. I wish there was more I could do for Bailey, but as it stands, I have exhausted all our options. All I have to offer Bailey is a mother's love and support. I love you, Bailey, and I am sorry I can't help you," Mrs. Taylor says as she walks off the podium.

Sobbing uncontrollably, she heads straight to the women's restroom. The room suddenly feels heavy with a strong emotional presence. Mothers themselves, the women in the group all sympathize with Mrs. Taylor's plight. Beth, a very close friend of the Taylors, pursues Mrs. Taylor to the restroom. She gives her a hug, trying to soothe her pain. Mrs. Taylor, feeling better, wipes her tears and is ready to join the others for the rest of the meeting. Just before Beth opens the restroom door, she stops.

"This is obviously hard for you to deal with. I truly am sorry for Bailey. But, Elizabeth, I need you to hear me out. Jeremy and I have started a swim school. We have very good instructors, and I think Bailey would like it. Why don't you bring her over? If she doesn't like her first week of lessons, you will not have to pay a penny for the classes," Beth says, gazing intently into Mrs. Taylor's eyes.

While listening to Beth, Mrs. Taylor had been about to blow up but somehow kept her cool and paid attention until she was finished. Mrs. Taylor feels let down by Beth, who she feels is being inconsiderate.

Seeing that Mrs. Taylor has remained speechless, Beth adds on, "I know it is cynical for me to suggest another swim school experience for Bailey after what happened. But I want you to take a leap of faith on this one."

"I guess there is no harm in trying; we have nothing to lose at this point as all the harm that could have been done to Bailey has already been done," Mrs. Taylor responds sheepishly. They both go back to take their seats to finish up with the fellowship.

CHAPTER 4

NOTHING SHALL BE IMPOSSIBLE

"WITH GOD, NOTHING SHALL BE IMPOSSIBLE," KWAMI speaks out loud to himself several times as he heads out for his interview at the swim school.

He follows up his confessions with worship songs, very hopeful that things are only going to get better from this point on. Just as his directional map suggested, he gets there in exactly thirty minutes and walks in confidently for his interview. He is asked about his work experience with lifeguarding, whether he has any form of certification, and if he loves working with children. Kwami does have some experience with lifeguarding, and he loves working with kids, but his current certification has expired, which is a major problem. All the same, he lets them know this, and at the end of the interview, he is told to come back and get trained for two weeks, after which a final decision will be made on whether or not he will be given the position.

Kwami comes in for his two-week training. He is trained by another lifeguard, who teaches him all that he needs to know in the first week and gives him the opportunity to show what he has learned in the second. It's unknown what feedback his trainer gives, but whatever it is, Kwami is given the job and able to start work right away.

Six months go by, and Kwami is excited about how things have been going when he is called into a meeting with his boss. Remembering his past experience at the restaurant, fear grips him, and his stomach begins to turn. He reflects on the many nights he had no money to buy food to eat and asks himself, "Why me?" To make matters worse, Kwami notices a second lady in the office. He recognizes her as she has come to the office many times, and his colleagues have said she is the owner of the swim school, but he didn't know whether to believe them or not. Well, here she is with his supervisor, looking very serious. Kwami knocks on their door and is asked to come in and take a sit, which he does with his legs wobbling. His supervisor, Lori, says hi, and the second lady does as well and introduces herself as Beth, the owner of the swim school. Now this makes Kwami cringe even more—it smells like trouble all over the room.

"Hi, Kwami," Lori says with a cheerful grin on her face.

Before Kwami can utter a response, Beth begins to speak. "Hello, Kwami, it's a pleasure meeting you."

Kwami hesitantly replies, "Likewise."

"You must be wondering why we brought you here," Lori continues.

Kwami with a hesitant look says nothing.

"Usually we do performance reviews for employees who have been working with us on a yearly basis, after which, we determine if they are deserving of a salary increment, a promotion, or if they need to be issued a caution. But with you, we are compelled to make an exemption. We are aware that you have only been with us for six months, but Beth and I have decided to give you a performance review of your work with us so far," Lori goes on to say.

"Kwami, we are impressed with your work so far. We have watched you closely, and let's just say that your smiles at the kids and how you interact with them is what we are very impressed about. Some of the parents of the kids have approached me and have shared how sweet and attentive you are with their children. I must say, we don't hear much of that about our lifeguards," Beth explains.

Lori interjects, "That being said, Beth and I have decided to promote you to head lifeguard. We will give you a raise, and we hope you will consider taking the position."

Elated, Kwami replies, "Yes! Yes! Please, I will take the position. Let me first of all say thank you for the opportunity to be here—I do not take it for granted. I love what I do, and I am glad everyone else appreciates my efforts."

Lori grins some more. "I know there is a class coming up, so that's it for now. Thanks for taking the position. We will take you through a few days of training, and you should be ready to resume your new position."

"Thank you," Kwami replies graciously.

Kwami leaves the office and goes straight to the washroom to change for the next class. When he notices no one there, he screams out a big, "Yes!" in excitement. He can't believe what just happened. Like Lori said, Kwami receives a week of training and becomes the head lifeguard of the swim school.

The summer is over, and most of the swim instructors, who are mostly college students, leave for their various colleges to start the fall semester, which leaves a huge gap in the number of swim instructors available to teach. Lori decides to get the lifeguards in the pool to be trained as swim instructors so that more kids can have lessons. This way, the school does not have to let kids go and lose money. Inevitably, Kwami needs to get into the pool to teach, but he hates the idea of being in the pool the whole day. He was comfortable where he was, but he has no choice. Training as a swim instructor is tedious for Kwami because there are a lot of techniques and skills he has to master to be able to teach well. This isn't fun for him at all. Soon enough, he is given his own classes to teach. He takes on his first class with ease but isn't sure if this is what he wants to be doing. However, he willingly offers to teach in the pool for as long as needed.

Like she does every other day, Beth walks onto the pool deck area out of the blue and watches Kwami for a good fifteen minutes while he is teaching.

She walks up to him and says, "How come all this time we never put you in the water to teach? You are a great teacher. Your place is not as a lifeguard—you need to be in the pool teaching!"

Kwami doesn't fully grasp what Beth has said until Lori comes out onto the pool deck area and lets him know that Beth is thinking about making him teach in the pool full time. Kwami can't believe his position is going to be changed again, but he is ready for the challenge. Lori presents him with his new classes, and his new position as a swim instructor starts with immediate effect.

CHANGE IS HERE

Mrs. Taylor is back from fellowship at midnight, and her husband is wide awake because Bailey has not been able to sleep. Tired as they both are, Mr. and Mrs. Taylor stay up all night with Bailey. While they are up, Mrs. Taylor mentions to Mr. Taylor about the conversation she had with Beth, who Mr. Taylor himself knows quite well. He also mentions to her how Jeremy, Beth's husband, had called him to check in on them. After Mr. Taylor shared with Jeremy about what had happened to Bailey, Jeremy suggested the same thing as his wife—that the Taylors give the new swim school Beth and Jeremy had just opened a try. Mr. and Mrs. Taylor remind themselves that they have nothing to lose but everything to gain if this works out. Beth and Jeremy's swim school has an indoor pool that is well-heated all year round. They decide to give Bailey some rest during the summer and enroll her in the fall.

The fall is here. Bailey gets a new pair of goggles and swimsuit so she is not reminded about her last swim experience. Mr. and Mrs. Taylor take Bailey to get registered and ask about who is going to be her teacher. They feel they need to ask because of their last experience. Kwami is confirmed as Bailey's new teacher. The name Kwami doesn't sound American, so the Taylors probe further and find out that he is from Africa and has only been teaching for the past ten months. This raises so many doubts in Mr. and Mrs. Taylor's minds. They question how effective he is going to be in communicating with Bailey, and being that he is the first person of color that Bailey will be in contact with, they wonder if she is going to freak out. But she has already been signed up for her classes, and there is no turning back at this point, so they just hope for the best.

Swim day is here, and Mom and Dad begin to prep Bailey for her first lesson. They prep her by telling her she is going to have the best swim instructor in the world and that if she gets through her first class without crying, they will buy her whatever she wants on the way home. They also tell her not to be scared because he has a different skin color, that he is just like her but a superhero from another planet, which makes Bailey smile. She is very excited to meet her superhero swim instructor.

FIRST WEEK

DAY 1

Bailey walks in with her new friend, who she has just met while waiting to come into class. They hold hands while walking to class together. Everything seems okay. Kwami gives them both along with his other two students a hug, and they all learn to sing a new song right. Bailey sings along, staring intensely at Kwami and turning to steal a glance at her parents, who are sitting behind a glass wall barrier separating them from the pool. She smiles at them, and they both respond with a thumbs up. It's Bailey's turn to swim, but as soon as Kwami grabs her, she screams and starts weeping profusely. Kwami carries her on his arms in hopes of calming her down, but this proves futile. Bailey goes through her first class without ever having her turn. Her parents are worried at this point, but they are certainly happy that she was able to sit through the class. Unfortunately, Bailey does not want to go back the next day, but her parents are able to convince her to give it another try to see how things turn out.

DAY 2

It's the second day, and Bailey starts weeping before she can even make it to the Kwami's class. Kwami starts talking to her, hoping to get a response back, but Bailey won't say anything. Missing her turns again, Kwami allows her to stay and watch the other kids swim and says very little back to her. Swim class is over, and Bailey walks out in a haste to get changed and leave.

DAY 3

The third day is here, and Bailey comes in crying again. At this point, Kwami gives her a hug but doesn't give her a turn at all. She is only allowed to watch her friends swim and take their turns.

DAY 4

The fourth day has come so quickly, and Bailey is the only one getting nothing out of her classes. She comes in crying, but not as much as before. Kwami notices this and tries to get her to learn a few new things, but she still won't try anything. As frustrating as it is, Kwami keeps his cool and allows Bailey to be herself.

DAY 5

Day 5 is here, the last day of Bailey's first week of swim classes. Kwami prepares hard for this day. He gets new toys and some tips from his supervisor about how to handle Bailey. It's time for class, and this time, Kwami hears no weeping but just sees tears in her eyes. He hopes today will be different, but it doesn't turn out that way. No number of toys or swim techniques Kwami uses can get Bailey to do some swimming.

Mr. and Mrs. Taylor are frustrated. Even though they are happy that Bailey got to see how fun swimming was for the other kids, it bothers them that she is not learning anything herself. Mrs. Taylor gives Beth a call and tells her about how things have gone so far with Bailey. Beth encourages her to keep bringing Bailey until she is finished with every one of her two weeks of classes. But this time, Beth promises to reschedule another swim instructor for Bailey, specifically a female instructor, to see if Bailey will respond better.

SECOND WEEK

DAY 1

Kwami is told over the weekend that Bailey will be changing classes. This saddens Kwami a tiny bit, but he knows he was not making any head way with her, so she deserves to get the help she needs. It is time for class, but for some reason, Bailey has come back to Kwami's class again. Kwami, a little confused, looks to his right across at the female instructor who Bailey is supposed to be with, but her class is full. He calls for the deck manager to look into it, and he comes back to say that Kwami is Bailey's teacher. Bailey's parents are equally confused, so they get the lifeguard on duty to get Bailey out of the pool. They go up to the front desk to check what is going on, and the schedule still has Kwami placed to teach Bailey. For some unknown reason, the change Beth suggested has not been done, and nothing can be done about it as the female instructor already has a fully booked class. So, Bailey has to stick with Kwami.

At this time, there has been so much confusion as to where Bailey belonged that fifteen minutes of her thirty-minute class have already gone by. Bailey's parents come over to apologize for taking her out of the pool for that long. Kwami apologizes back for the confusion, and they both agree to give it another try the next day.

Day 2

Day 2 of the second week is here. Kwami is convinced he is going to have Bailey for the rest of her classes. He is out of options on how to help her, and at this point, he is mad at his supervisors for not rescheduling Bailey's class because he is certain she is not going to get the help she needs. Here we go again—Bailey comes walking in slowly, dragging her feet with wandering eyes as though she has a lot on her mind.

"Hi, Mr. Kwami," Bailey says without a smile.

Kwami turns to look at Bailey as if he has just seen a ghost. He can't believe Bailey just spoke to him!

"Hi, Bailey," Kwami eagerly responds, smiling back at her in disbelief.

They give each other a warm hug.

"Would you like to try blowing your bubbles with me?" Kwami asks politely.

"No! Mr. Kwami let Ashley (who is standing next to her) go," Bailey responds in a haste.

"Okay, I will come to you after I am done with her," Kwami explains.

Kwami is done with Ashley and returns back to Bailey.

"Bailey, ready?" he says, stretching his hands to grab hers.

"No! Mr. Kwami let the other two have their turns, and then I will go," Bailey replies in a soft tone.

"Bailey! After these two, if we have to skip your turn again, you are going to break my heart," Kwami says, looking straight into her eyes.

It doesn't look like she cares too much, but it was a good try by Kwami. The other two have their equal turns, and Bailey looks like her world is coming to end.

Kwami whispers, "Bailey! I just need you to blow your bubbles for four seconds. I am going to count, 'One, two, three, and four,' and at the fourth count, I want you to lift your head and breathe."

"Mr. Kwami, I can only do two seconds," Bailey replies.

"Bailey, I believe you can do four seconds. All your friends have done it, and so can you," Kwami responds.

Bailey, looking like she is about to cry, cries out, "Can we do it for two seconds?"

"Okay, sure!" Kwami agrees. "Please don't cry. Let's do only two seconds," Kwami says, reaching out to hold Bailey in his arms.

To everyone's amazement, Bailey goes over to him. Kwami grabs firmly onto her waist and puts her on her tummy. Bailey dips her face halfway into the water and blows her bubbles for two seconds.

"Bailey! That was awesome! I am so proud of you. Let's try our flutter kicks with the barbells all the way to the other side," Kwami says while clapping his hands.

"No! I can't do it all the way to the other side," Bailey responds.

"Can we try just halfway, please?" Kwami asks convincingly.

"Just halfway, Mr. Kwami," Bailey says softly.

Bailey, again to everyone's amazement, grabs onto the barbell and practices her flutter kicks halfway and back.

"Now, let's try doing the two together!" Kwami says excitedly.

"No, I can't do the two together," Bailey replies.

At this point, Kwami is beside himself with joy but decides not to push it so he doesn't ruin it for her. He wants her to catch up with her friends so badly because she has only three days before lessons are over, and it took her friends a whole week to learn to combine both swim techniques.

DAY 3

Bailey walks in with wandering eyes again, almost hesitant to come to class.

"Hi, Mr. Kwami," she says.

"Hi, Bailey. Bailey, would you like the others to have their turn before you do?" Kwami suggests.

"Yes!" Bailey screams out loud.

Not a surprising answer, but the scream confirms how serious Bailey is.

"Bailey, everyone has had their turn. Let's practice blowing our bubbles for…" Before Kwami can finish getting the words out of his mouth, Bailey interjects.

"Two seconds! Two seconds!" she screams.

"Okay, Bailey! Two seconds it is," Kwami replies.

But this time, Kwami decides to push Bailey a little bit more. He helps her blow her bubbles for two seconds and loosens his hold on her immediately, letting her go a little deeper into the water and counting to the fourth second before bringing her back up. Bailey comes back up crying.

"Bailey! What happened? Did you just blow your bubbles for four seconds? Yay! I'm very proud of you!" Kwami shouts with joy, turning heads.

"You let me go! You said we were only doing two seconds. You let me go!" Bailey says, crying a little harder.

"Bailey! I let you go because I believed you could do it. I believe in you, Bailey. I want you to believe in yourself," Kwami whispers.

"I don't want to swim again," Bailey replies with folded arms.

Kwami ignores her and gives the other kids their turns practicing their flutter kicks. Kwami comes back to Bailey, who still has her arms folded.

"Bailey, I'm sorry. Let's practice our kicks halfway. It will be so quick that you won't even know it happened," Kwame says, trying hard to win back her trust.

Bailey still has her arms folded, but Kwami is not having it this time. He unfolds them gently and puts them over the barbell, and off Bailey goes, kicking from one end of the pool to the other. Before they know it, there are sounds of applause all around from the other swim instructors to the lifeguards on duty, and Kwami eventually joins in as he watches her parents tear up with admiration at what has just happened. They all can't believe she made it all the way to the end of the pool and back.

"That's my father and my mother!" Bailey says with a smile and a thumbs up pointing at them.

"Yes, Bailey, that is Mom and Dad. They are very proud of you," Kwami responds, holding back tears.

"Yes, they are," Bailey murmurs.

Swim class is over, and Bailey runs into her parents' arms, this time with a lot of joy.

DAY 4

It is the day before the last, and Kwami is happy about the progress Bailey has made but is worried she might not learn enough before her classes are over. But look who comes dashing into class five minutes early, just as Kwami is closing his previous class.

"Hi, Mr. Kwami!" she shouts from a distance as she runs in.

"Hi, Bailey!" Kwami shouts back as everyone turns around and stares at them both. Bailey stands there for five minutes waiting for Kwami's class to be done and runs over to give him a hug. Soon after, her friends join in, and the class begins. As expected, Kwami decides to start the others before coming to Bailey, but this time, just as Kwami is about to start with Ashley, Bailey puts her hand up, shouting "Me! Me! Me!" Kwami, still very amazed but very happy, allows Bailey to have her turn first.

"Bailey, are you going to be first today?" Kwami asks.

"Yes!" she replies.

"Okay! That's very good. Now let's do our two-second count with bubbles, okay?" Kwami goes on to say.

"No! Let's do four seconds. I will blow bubbles in the water, and you will count, 'One, two, three, four,' and I will lift my head up at four, okay!" she instructs, almost ready to jump into the water without the usual tussle.

"Okay! Bailey, look at you go!" Kwami responds.

She blows her bubbles for four seconds and lifts her head up with a smile on her face. Kwami gives her a high five. Just as Kwami is going to give the others a turn, Bailey puts up her hand again.

"Bailey, what's wrong?" Kwami asks.

"I want to show you my flutter kicks. Don't hold the barbells anymore. I will do it by myself!" Bailey goes on instructing.

"Are you going all the way by yourself?" Kwami asks, shocked.

"Yes! Yes! Yes!" Bailey screams. With every yes, her voice grows louder.

Bailey literally jumps onto the barbell, and off she goes while Kwami watches attentively and cheers her on all the way.

"Woohoo! Good job, Bailey! I am super proud of you," Kwami tells her.

Kwami is finally able to give everyone a turn and bring class to an end.

DAY 5

The last day of swim classes is here. This is the day Bailey and her other swim mates show Kwami all they have learned in the past two weeks. It is also a big day for the kids because their parents get to come to the pool deck area and watch first-hand how they are doing. So, of course, Bailey's parents are there, sitting right behind her. Bailey is so ready to go, putting up her hands at every instance she gets. She does every one of the lessons with ease, and even more surprisingly, she is able to do both her kicks and bubbles together, which is the ultimate goal to be able to go on to the next class. This wows her parents, who can't believe their eyes. Every one of Kwami's students passes the class, but what makes Bailey stand out that day is that while everyone else took two weeks to master their lessons, Bailey did so in three days.

After class, everyone is awarded a certificate. Bailey's parents stay to have a chat with Kwami.

"Mr. Kwami, we really appreciate all that you have done for Bailey. We can't believe the amount of progress she has made," Mrs. Taylor says.

"You are welcome, Mrs. Taylor. Bailey is an amazing kid," Kwami responds.

"How long are you going to be here?" Mrs. Taylor proceeds to ask.

"Not long, Mrs. Taylor. I will be leaving for Ghana, my home country, in about three weeks. I am only here for school, and I graduate in two weeks," Kwame replies.

"Oh, congratulations! We wish you could be here forever. Can Bailey have one more week with you? She doesn't want to have swim classes if it is not with you," Mrs. Taylor says, giving Bailey a kiss on the head.

"Yes, sure. I would love to have her for another week. Hopefully we make a lot more progress," Kwami responds cheerfully.

"Thanks, Kwami," Mr. Taylor says, and they both exchange a firm handshake.

CHAPTER 5

THE FINAL WORK

KWAMI HAS BAILEY AGAIN FOR ANOTHER WEEK, AND IT turns out to be the best week he has ever had with a student. Bailey learns how to freestyle swim and has close-to-perfect strokes. Her breath control is amazing, her kicks are great, and she is able to swim from one end of the pool to another without any assistance. As a result, Kwami becomes the go-to instructor for kids who have had any form of trauma and fear of swimming, and they all show great improvement. He is the favorite swim instructor for many kids and has so many shout-outs from kids and parents that they cannot all fit under his name on the shout-out board! But all too soon, he has to bid everyone farewell. His stay in America has come to an end. Kwami is looking forward to going back home, even though he has been so successful at school and work. On his last day at work, when he goes into his swim instructor file to discard whatever is left of his belongings, he finds an envelope which is unusually bigger than the ones he normally gets from parents. It reads "Mr. Kwami" on the front, so he knows it is definitely his. He takes it home with the intention of reading it later on that night, but when he gets home, he has to pack and clean his dorm and is way too tired to read the letter.

It is his last day in America, and Kwami takes one good look at his dorm room, gets his bags, and catches an Uber to the airport. It's a forty-minute ride, so Kwami has some time and decides to read the mysterious letter. He opens the sealed envelope, unfolds the letter, and reads:

"Hello, Mr. Kwami,

We just want to say how blessed we are to know you and to have had you as Bailey's swim teacher. We must say we were very skeptical about how well Bailey would do with swim classes. She had a very traumatizing experience with her last swim instructor, and after two days of having you as her swim instructor, she didn't want to continue with swim classes. We saw how much she cried all throughout the first week. But you were very patient and kind to her. We were very shocked, as we assume you were too, when she started participating in class.

Not only did you get her to participate, but she is actually now swimming all by herself. We couldn't be any prouder. But you have become more than a swim teacher to Bailey. At one point of her life, Bailey became very timid and reserved. She never wanted to go out of the house and shied away from any activity that would force her to do so. We paid a child psychologist a visit about Bailey's problem, and all she said was that we should give it time. But as time passed, her condition worsened. After Bailey's last week with you, she has become a whole new person. She rides her bicycle now and will jump the wall and go play with her friends. She even wants to get her ears pierced, something we have struggled to get her to do for some time now. She never wanted to take a shower, but now she does so without freaking out as well as sleep with the lights off. She has become confident and fearless. Thank you for giving us back our daughter; we honestly thought we had lost her. We wish you all the best on your endeavors back home, and we know you will do well in whatever you do. Please let us know if there is any form of help you need from us.

Mr. and Mrs. Taylor.

Blinded with tears in his eyes, Kwami almost stumbles out of the Uber, trying to quickly wipe them away. He checks his bags in, quickly goes through TSA, and boards the plane home. As he takes his assigned seat, he begins to reminisce about his time in America. He remembers the cold winters, the long journeys he had to make to his first job, surviving off meals on credit, the night he had nothing to eat at all, getting a new job, and meeting all the wonderful kids whose lives he changed, especially Bailey's.

It also begins to dawn on him how much of Bailey he sees in himself. Growing up, for a very long time, he too could not sleep with the lights off. For many years, Kwami wrestled with many internal struggles, but his internal fears superseded them all. They were so significant that they had affected his social life. If there were any two words that described Kwami's personality, they would be reserved and quiet.

"If Bailey can do it, I also can," Kwami repeats to himself many times over and over again, while he thinks about his own fears.

As he gets deeper in his thoughts, a song called "Blessings" by Laura Story keeps coming back to him. This is one of his favorite songs that he heard on a radio station called K-Love, which he would tune in to anytime he was driving. With a soft whisper, he sings under his breath as the plane home goes shooting into the sky.

Today, Kwami has been able to do so much with his own life, things he never imagined could be possible. Bailey did not only give Kwami the courage to overcome his fears, but through her, he found his life's purpose. After a year and half in Ghana, Kwami came back to America and got a job at the Kennedy Krieger Institute in Maryland as an adapted aquatics specialist, where he works with children with special needs in the pool. I know this because I am Kwami, and I am who I am today because of my encounter with Bailey. This is my testimony.

Final Words

"I have told you these things, so that in Me you may have [perfect] peace. In the world you have tribulation and distress and suffering, but be courageous [be confident, be undaunted, be filled with joy]; I have overcome the world." — *John 16:33 (AMP)*

Dear reader, we live in very difficult and uncertain times, and you may equally be going through difficult times in life as well. I want you to know that you are not alone. Jesus reminds us in John 16:33 that in this life there will be moments of tribulations, distress, and suffering, but be encouraged because He has overcome the world, and so can you.

He came right to the point and said, "I want to give you (and this is HIS expression) an 'overlay' of truth." In a split second of eternity, we went from Genesis to Revelation, looking first at God's plan for his people. Throughout the entire Bible, God dis-cussed his character, stating I will do nothing in conflict with my nature or my character. My plan for you is good and it will be accomplished." He referred me to Jeremiah 29:11, "For I know the thoughts that I think toward you, saithe the Lord, thoughts of peace, and not of evil, to give you an expected end." In giving me these thoughts, God wanted me to see how he really felt about man; that he had man in mind before he made the earth; and he made the earth so man would have a place on which to live. When he looks at man, he does not look at the evil, which has taken place, but he looks at the very heart of man.

Then God said I could ask questions! My mind was whirling! How does a human ask questions of God? It was so awesome being in his presence I could hardly think. Finally, a thought came into my mind to find out whether or not he actually made individual plans for each and every life, because for some reason or other, I felt this gigantic task would be too big even for God!

In answer to my question, God let me see the vast-ness of his heavenly archives! My head swam! There was no way my finite mind could understand how God could keep track of these files. There must be bil-lions of them! He said, "Since you are overwhelmed by this, and it staggers you, let me pull out one that you can relate to." And he immediately pulled out mine! He would not let me see the contents of it, but mentioned a few of the future items listed which I could use as confirmation of this visit.

Then he did another very surprising thing! He wrote down 120 events, which he said would happen in my life in the future…

He said, "Let me show you someone else's record that you will easily understand." He pulled out the file on Cyrus and reminded me of the last verse of Isaiah 44, and the first five verses of 45 where he said, "When I say of Cyrus, 'He is my shepherd,' he will certainly do as I say; and Jerusalem will be rebuilt and the Temple restored, for I have spoken it." This is Jehovah's message to Cyrus, God's anointed, whom he has chosen to conquer many lands. God shall empower his right hand and he shall crush the strength of mighty kings. God shall open the gates of Babylon to him; the gates shall not be shut against him anymore. I will go before you, Cyrus, and level the mountains and smash down the city gates of brass and iron bars. And I will give you treasures hidden in the darkness, secret riches; and you will know that I am doing this, I, the Lord, the God of Israel, the one who calls you by your name. "And why have I named you for this work? For the sake of Jacob, my servant Israel, my chosen. I called you by name when you didn't know me" (TLB). God looked far into the future and saw exactly what was going to happen.

He allowed me to see the record books, and also his blueprints for many lives. One book was that of the apostle Paul. It revealed that he would be used to bring the Gospel to kings, rulers, and men of authority. For this reason, God gave him a bigger brain capacity than normal, and because he was more brilliant, he caused him to study under the greatest teachers of his day, finally being tutored by Gamaliel, the most outstanding teacher of that time. God had chosen Paul to write the Scripture, the Epistles, His plan for the church and His body, so he prepared him for this task.

…God emphasized to me that we should quit worrying about HIS responsibilities. He actually lets me view people who are trying to serve him by seeing how much they can get their minds in tune with him, by trying to think just exactly right, or trying to say the right word at the right time! God emphasized to me, "That is my business. You worship me, walk with me, put your hand in mine, get your heart in tune with me and I will give you the privilege of moving with me.

"Let me take care of my own business! What I have promised is my business, and I will take care of it. I have not failed in all of this time. Not even one of my words has failed in all of my good promises." [1]

The above script is an excerpt taken from chapter 4 of Pastor Roland Buck's book *Angels on Assignment*, titled "My visit to the throne room." In this chapter, he narrates how on one Saturday night in January of 1977, at about 10:30 pm, he

---

[1] Angels on Assignment by Charles and Frances Hunter, as told by Roland Buck (1979)

was seated at his desk, meditating, praying, and preparing his heart for Sunday. He had his head down on his arms when suddenly, he was taken right out of that room. He heard a voice say, "Come with Me into the throne room where the secrets of the universe are kept!"

From the above excerpt, you will notice that God continued to say, "I want to give you an 'overlay' of truth," taking him from Genesis to Revelation, looking first at God's plan for His people. God has always put His plans for you first before anything else. God went on to tell him, "My plan for you is good, and it will be accomplished." This is also true about us today. God has a plan for you, and not only is it good, but it will be accomplished. It is such great news that God will not leave us helpless. He has a plan for whatever situation we may be going through. Even when our challenges persist, remember that He is committed to accomplishing His will for us.

In the same chapter, God gave Pastor Roland Buck the opportunity to ask questions. He asked God whether or not He actually made individual plans for each and every life. In God's answer to Pastor Buck's question, God let him see the vastness of His heavenly archives! Pastor Buck went on to narrate that there was no way his finite mind could understand how God could keep track of these files because there were billions of them! Your file, dear reader, is amongst the many billions of files in heaven. God went on to say to him, "Since you are overwhelmed by this and it staggers you, let Me pull out one that you can relate to." And God immediately pulled out Pastor Roland Buck's own file. He would not let him see the contents of it but mentioned a few of the future items listed which Pastor Buck could use as confirmation of his visit.

Then God did another very surprising thing! He wrote down 120 events which He said would happen in Pastor Buck's life in the future. Dear reader, what if God gave you 120 events that would happen in your future—would that put your mind at ease? Would you then see that there is joy after the tears, hope in the midst of uncertainty, and peace after the storm? Well, the good news is that those 120 events and more are already written, and they will all happen as planned. God allowed Pastor Buck to see the records and blueprints of many lives, including that of Cyrus and Apostle Paul. What he found interesting about the blueprint of Apostle Paul is how, apart from revealing his purpose, God gave Paul the physical capabilities (a bigger brain capacity than normal) necessary and prepared him (tutored by Gamaliel, the most outstanding teacher of that time) to fulfil his purpose. Take a good look around you and at yourself—everything you see is an indication of God's plan at work, even the difficulties. With regards to God's plans and promise, God emphasized to Pastor Roland Buck that we should quit worrying about His responsibilities and that all He really wants from us is our worship, to walk with Him, put our hand in His, and get our heart in tune with His. He finally said to him, "Let Me take care of My own business! What I have promised is My business, and I will take care of it. I have not failed in all of this time. Not even one of My words has failed in all of My good promises."

Dear reader, a lot of us are trying to figure out life by ourselves, and in doing so, we put ourselves into even more trouble. Until God shows you His plans for you, what you see and know about your situation and how to get out of it will always be very limited and skewed. Blessings don't always look or come in the form or fashion we expect them to. They are usually disguised in a little pain or sorrow, moments of tears, or hard and difficult times. Just because things are not panning out the way they should doesn't mean we should take things into our hands. God has a blueprint for your life, and every plan inside of it is good. It is His responsibility to see them through, not yours. Don't give up, and don't give in; hold on a little longer. Trust His plan for your life, and you will have a hope and a future.

Mr. Kwami teaching a student, summer 2016

About the Author

E LI K. ANYADI, A HUSBAND AND A FATHER, IS A Christian author based in Maryland, who was born and raised in Ghana, West Africa. He moved to the US permanently after pursuing an MBA degree in healthcare management and is passionate about shepherding young adults to be better Christians

CPSIA information can be obtained
at www.ICGtesting.com
Printed in the USA
BVHW060250110821
614046BV00005B/63

9 781662 823046